BEN SHAHN
PHOTOGRAPHER

BEN SHAHN
PHOTOGRAPHER

An Album from the Thirties

Edited, with an Introduction, by Margaret R. Weiss

DA CAPO PRESS · New York · 1973

Ben Shahn, Photographer, is published by arrangement with the estate of the
artist. The photographs have been reproduced from originals provided by the
Shahn estate and by the Prints and Photographs Division, Library of Congress.
Captions are based on information in the files of the Farm Security
Administration Collection, Library of Congress. Design of the volume follows
suggestions offered by Bernarda Bryson Shahn and by Walker Evans. Except for
the photograph reproduced on the end papers, the full image of each picture, as
received by the publisher, has been retained.

Library of Congress Cataloging in Publication Data

Shahn, Ben, 1898-1969.
  Ben Shahn, photographer.

  1. Photography, Artistic. 2. United States—Description and travel—Views. 3. United States.
Farm Security Administration. I. Weiss, Margaret R., ed. II. Title.
TR653.S5 1973 779'.9'9173039160924 77-75271
ISBN 0-306-71312-8

Design: Elliot Epstein
Manufactured in the United States of America

Published by Da Capo Press, Inc.
A Subsidiary of Plenum Publishing Corporation
227 West 17th Street
New York, New York 10011

INTRODUCTION

Though the biographers and bibliographers of Ben Shahn have been busy over the years recording his achievements as a painter, muralist, graphic artist, and illustrator, one aspect of his creative experience has been glossed over. This was the period in the mid-thirties when his camera proved to be a major item in his economic survival kit during the Depression years.

Shahn already had behind him successful one-man shows of his controversial series, *The Passion of Sacco and Vanzetti* and *The Mooney Case*, as well as representation in a group exhibition of murals at The Museum of Modern Art, when he decided to enroll with the government-sponsored Public Works of Art Project in 1934. After a year of committee-spawned frustrations which left in limbo the murals intended for Central Park's casino and for the Rikers Island penitentiary, his talents in graphic art and design were absorbed into the Special Skills Division of the Resettlement Administration (subsequently rechristened the Farm Security Administration).

Doubtless spurred by his friend Walker Evans, the photographer with whom he had earlier shared a studio in Greenwich Village, Shahn soon transferred to the Historical Section of the Division of Information—a purely Federalese label for a camera unit that was to write its own chapter of photographic history. Under the dynamic, at times evangelistic direction of Roy E. Stryker, a dozen FSA photographers—Walker Evans, Dorothea Lange, Russell Lee, Carl Mydans, Arthur Rothstein, and Ben Shahn, among them—produced some 270,000 negatives documenting the life pattern of the "starved, stalled and stranded" in a rural America atrophied by acute economic paralysis.

As part of the FSA unit, the artist-turned-photographer accepted the challenge of Stryker's directive "to know enough about the subject matter, to find its significance in itself and in relation to the surroundings, its time and its function." Between 1935 and 1938, on trips that lasted four or five months at a stretch, Shahn's $6-per-diem-and-5¢-a-mile-for-gas took him all through the South and Midwest: into the farmlands and main streets of Ohio, the Carolinas, and Tennessee; into the mining towns and railroad yards of West Virginia and Kentucky; into Arkansas squatters' huts and cottonpickers' lean-tos; into Ozark schoolrooms; into the homes of Louisiana trappers and tenant farmers.

His Leica—small, unobstrusive, equipped with a right-angle viewfinder that allowed him to capture his subjects unaware—was an ideal traveling companion. What only a few years before had seemed to him no more than a fascinating toy became a facile tool—a mechanical recording angel capable of making a "sketchbook" of on-the-spot images rich in precise detail. There was much about a camera that Shahn found appealing. It was a fairly reliable reporter, and it could freeze split-second action. It was direct and straightforward in approach; it made the everyday and commonplace compelling. It could catch the textures and planes revealed by the interplay of light and shadow—the "shape of content" with which Shahn the photographer was as much concerned as Shahn the artist.

The transition from amateur to professional lensman may well have occurred when Shahn was collaborating with Lou Block on plans for the Rikers Island mural. Sharing the assignment, the two men also shared the preparatory step of taking their cameras to Manhattan's Lower East Side and to many of New York's prisons in order to shoot "character" studies of city-street types. Both as a convenient research-gathering method and as a dependable *aide-mémoire*, visual notetaking such as this satisfied Shahn's penchant for careful documentation.

In painting, his passion for precision was reinforced by his early study of the Florentine and Sienese masters; his preference for sharply contrasting realistic and stylized forms burgeoned under exposure to Diego Rivera's work. In photography, he admired the direct field photojournalism of Mathew Brady, the compassionate lens of Lewis Hine, the unerring craftsmanship of Walker Evans, and the consummate blend of all three that he had found in the camerawork of the young Henri Cartier-Bresson as early as 1933.

Except for the catalogue annotator, it is an unrewarding task to subdivide and dissect an artist's work according to the media in which at various times he elects to render his visual impressions. For the creative impulse—that elusive union of sight and insight—the medium is not the message. And for Shahn, his six thousand FSA photographs were pictures, not paper images. Whether he put his impressions on film, canvas, or plaster wall, his artistic purpose was the creation of an evocative document that would recall in tranquillity an intensely felt response to some sector of the human environment or experience.

What pleased Shahn most about the camera was its unique ability to preserve the ephemeral—a fleeting image, a fragment of feeling, a fraction of time. To be sure, the picture elements would have to be framed in an ordered relationship before what was originally seen and felt could be translated into a quickly comprehended visual vocabulary. Here, the artist's trained eye would have its advantage as an instant translator and interpreter.

Conceding to a *U.S. Camera* reporter in 1946 that his interest in photography was primarily "to make notes for future paintings," Shahn certainly had a more immediate motivation during the FSA period of his career. Other observations he shared in that interview, however, reveal a consistent attitude toward all his image-making: "I paint or photograph for two reasons—either because I like certain events, things or people with great intensity or because I dislike others with equal intensity. I try to give my photographs and paintings as much of this intensity as I know how...."; "In photography, I'm interested in recording essentials, the essentials of form—the unessentials I crop in printing...."; "I never think about composition when I shoot. If my photographs have what is called composition, then that is so much velvet."

Characteristically, he believed that an artist's identity was ineffably linked to self-awareness and affirmation. For him, "as is" rather than "as if" was the keystone of his credo. Even as a young painter (with two extensive trips abroad already behind him), he

wanted to shed European stylistic influences and relate to his own time and place. Recalling years later what had been a turning-point in his professional life, he said: "I got to thinking about the Sacco-Vanzetti case.... Ever since I could remember I wished that I had been lucky enough to be alive when something big was going on, like the Crucifixion. And suddenly I realized I was. Here I was living through another crucifixion. Here was something to paint!" By 1935 "something big" was going on throughout America—the daily miracle of survival in a rural landscape immobilized by drought, dust, and deprivation. Here, indeed, was something to *photograph* —and Shahn was among the first to do so as part of Roy Stryker's unit.

Recently reviewing some of the Shahn photographs, Stryker admitted that he found it difficult to pinpoint exactly what earmarked them for special attention. "But something happens there in those pictures. Maybe it was in the wonderful tolerance, sympathy and feeling he had for people—for human beings. He said, 'I talk to them...I like them. I like people—and maybe they knew I liked them.' Ben was a man of great experience—a man with a sense of life. He knew about lots of things...he knew about people. I believe that he did have the ability to reach out and reach into individuals by his nature, his manner, his approach when he was taking pictures. In some way people opened up. They opened up and said, 'Here we are.' Looking at his pictures, one is sure that he related to those people and knew something about what was going on in their minds and troubled lives. His pictures project a sense of place, but not necessarily any particular locale. You know one scene is in a town, another is out in the country. All are part of a period which reflected an economic and social attitude born of hard times."

The photographer himself would probably have agreed with much of this analysis. In his own evaluation of what the FSA assignment meant to him, however, he preferred to focus on the effect it had on his painting. Assessing the post-World War II directions of art—his own included—he acknowledged that "for me the change had begun during the time when I worked in the Resettlement Administration [FSA]. I had then crossed and recrossed many sections of the country, and had come to know well so many people of all kinds of belief and temperament, which they maintained with a transcendent indifference to their lot in life. Theories had melted before such experience. My own painting then had turned from what is called 'social realism' into a sort of personal realism. I found the qualities of people a constant pleasure.... There were the poor who were rich in spirit, and the rich who were also sometimes rich in spirit."

Never underestimating the usefulness of photography as a visual aid to his painting, Shahn had no pretensions about his technical camera skills. In response to a question once put to him by my friend and colleague Katharine Kuh, he quickly replied, "I was not trained as a photographer. I took it [photography] up to help me sharpen my vision of the specific. I felt very strongly that I could arrive at broad generalizations about human beings through sharpened observation of the specific. For example, for the painting called *Handball* I made many photos of handball players in the slum playgrounds of New York."

James Thrall Soby, the artist's most dependable biographer, has noted that many of his paintings were "imaginative reconstructions of snapshots which he—or occasionally others—had taken." The election poster which appears in the painting *Sunday Football* was a realistic detail that Shahn borrowed intact from his poster-picture file. *Myself Among The Churchgoers* (in which he depicted) himself training his right-angle viewfinder on a scene that is a prototype of those he had seen and photographed many times during his FSA travels), *The Blind Accordion Player, Nearly Everybody Reads The Bulletin, East Twelfth Street, Welders, Ave*—any and all of these, as well as figures and configurations that reappear in some of the Shahn murals, are strongly derivative of his earlier camera subjects.

Pointing out such similarities has become a little game that critics like to play. But the fact that the artist was able to find multiple applications for his photographic images in no way diminishes their primary value as pictures. Rather, it heightens the realization that the inner eye continually transcends the arbitrary bonds of time and space in extracting the universal essence from the particulars of experience.

Though his camera was as adept at social comment as his brush, Shahn used the idiom of the lens less for stone-throwing at the Establishment than for making a personal statement about the human condition. To his way of seeing, man's world was an easily traceable graph of hapless ironies, of isolation amid overcrowding, of cold façades masking human warmth, of eyeless windows, of doors that opened only to vistas of barren desolation.

Whatever his indictments may have been, however, they were not without the leaven of humor or the salt of satire. His close-up of a photographer's window becomes a social register of the anonymous and uncelebrated of Main Street, U.S.A.; his Circleville, Ohio, scenes square the circle to let the viewer share in the charades of small-town life.

Ben Shahn believed that "it is the mission of art to remind man he is human." Sighting with a self-assigned "humble lens," he accomplished that mission as an FSA photographer. For he preserved on film a memorable—and unvarnished—camera portrait of rural America trapped in the inhumanities of the Thirties.

*　*　*　*

A Note of Acknowledgment

For their gracious sharing of reminiscences and research files, a full measure of appreciation goes to Bernarda B. Shahn, Roy E. Stryker, and Davis Pratt of the Carpenter Center for the Visual Arts, Harvard University.

M. R. W.

BEN SHAHN
PHOTOGRAPHER

STREET SCENE
Murfreesboro, Tennessee
October 1935

2

AMISH COUPLE
Plain City, Ohio
August 1938

3.

STREET SCENE
Circleville, Ohio
Summer 1938

STREET SCENE
Somerset, Ohio
Summer 1938

DRUGSTORE SIGN
Newark, Ohio
Summer 1938

STREET SCENE
Lancaster, Ohio
August 1938

A DEPUTY DURING THE STRIKE
Morgantown, West Virginia
September 1935

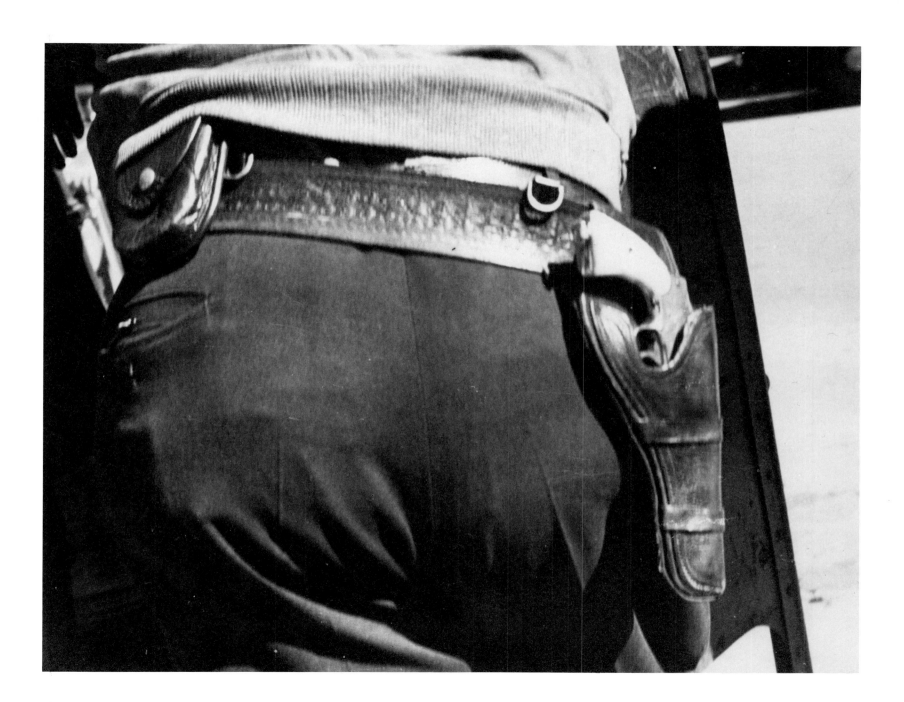

RESTAURANT WINDOW
Murfreesboro, Tennessee
October 1935

9.

STREET SCENE
Urbana, Ohio
August 1938

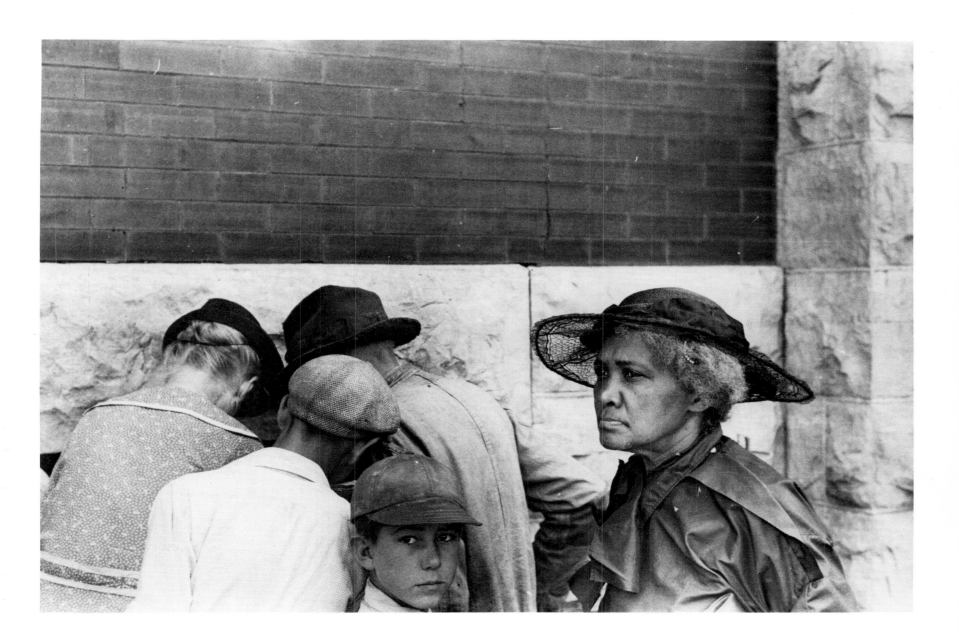

A YOUNG FAMILY
Smithland, Kentucky
October 1935

MAIN STREET
Plain City, Ohio
August 1938

12.

JULY 4TH CELEBRATION
Ashville, Ohio
1938

JULY 4TH CELEBRATION
Ashville, Ohio
1938

14.

SUNDAY
Little Rock, Arkansas
October 1935

15.

COUNTY FAIR
Central Ohio
August 1938

COUNTY FAIR
Central Ohio
August 1938

CARNIVAL
London, Ohio
Summer 1938

CIRCUS POSTER
Smithland, Kentucky
September 1935

ROADSIDE STOP
Central Ohio
Summer 1938

STREET SCENE
Natchez, Mississippi
October 1935

22.

UNEMPLOYED MINER
Scott's Run, West Virginia
October 1935

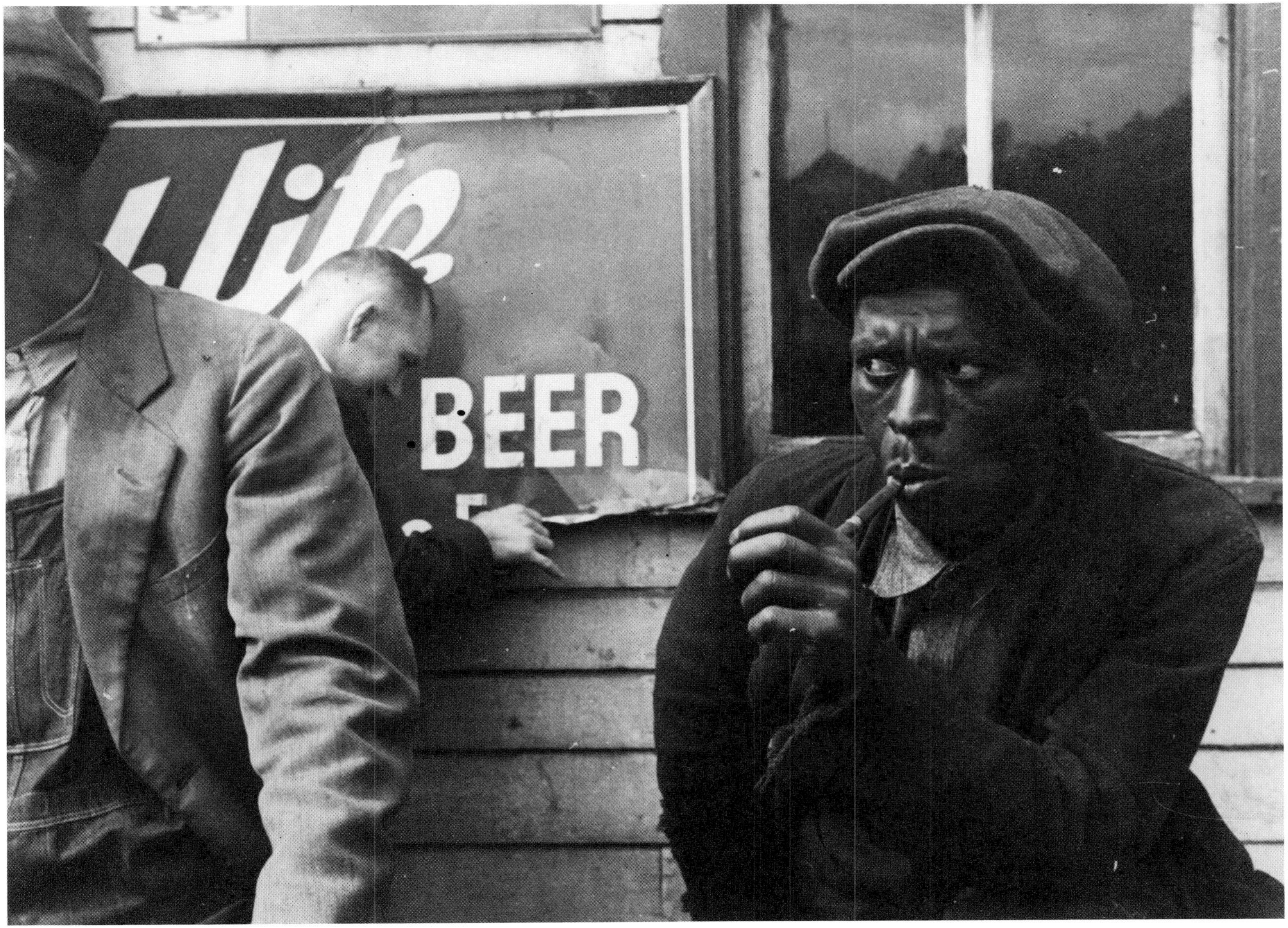
BEER

RELIGIOUS MEETING
Nashville, Tennessee
September 1935

MEDICINE SHOW
Huntingdon, Tennessee
October 1935

MEDICINE SHOW
Huntingdon, Tennessee
October 1935

SUNDAY
Scott's Run, West Virginia
October 1935

STREET SCENE
Huntingdon, Tennessee
October 1935

28.

COAL MINER
Kentucky
October 1935

29.

VIEW OF FREEZE FORK ON SCOTT'S RUN
West Virginia
October 1935

SALVAGING COAL FROM A SLAG HEAP
Nanty Glo, Pennsylvania
1937

31.

STRAWBERRY PICKER
Hammond, Louisiana
October 1935

STRAWBERRY PICKER'S HOME
Hammond, Louisiana
October 1935

HOME OF A DESTITUTE OZARK FAMILY
Arkansas
October 1935

SUNDAY
Omar, West Virginia
October 1935

35.

RAILROAD STATION
Circleville, Ohio
Summer 1938

THRESHING MACHINE
Pulaski County, Arkansas
October 1935

FAMILY ON RELIEF
Vicinity Urbana, Ohio
August 1938

HOOVERVILLE RESIDENT
Circleville, Ohio
Summer 1938

TENANT FARMER
Boone County, Arkansas
October 1935

40.
UNEMPLOYED CREOLE TRAPPER
Plaquemines Parish, Louisiana
October 1935

OZARK SHARECROPPER
Arkansas
October 1935

SHARECROPPER'S WIFE
Pulaski County, Arkansas
October 1935

43.

OZARK SHARECROPPER
Arkansas
October 1935

44.

SQUATTER'S HOME
Arkansas
October 1935

45.

OZARK COUPLE
Arkansas
October 1935

46.

OLD BARN ON U.S. 40
Central Ohio
Summer 1938

47.

ROADSIDE VIEW
Purseglove on Scott's Run, West Virginia
October 1935

48.

ON U.S. 40
Central Ohio
Summer 1938

49.

OZARK SCENE
Arkansas
October 1935

DESTITUTE OZARK FAMILY
Arkansas
October 1935

51.

DESTITUTE OZARK MOTHER AND CHILD
Arkansas
October 1935

52.

REHABILITATION CLIENTS
Boone County, Arkansas
October 1935

REHABILITATION CLIENT
Boone County, Arkansas
October 1935

REHABILITATION CLIENTS
Boone County, Arkansas
October 1935

DESTITUTE OZARK SHARECROPPER FAMILY
Arkansas
October 1935

56.

CHILDREN OF A DESTITUTE
OZARK SHARECROPPER
Arkansas
October 1935

DESTITUTE OZARK MOTHER AND CHILD
Arkansas
October 1935

CHILDREN OF A DESTITUTE
OZARK SHARECROPPER
Arkansas
October 1935

59.

CHILDREN
Arkansas
October 1935

FAMILY SCENE
Little Rock, Arkansas
October 1935

REHABILITATION CLIENT
Arkansas
October 1935

62.

CHILDREN
Arkansas
October 1935

CHILDREN OF A REHABILITATION CLIENT
Arkansas
October 1935

DAUGHTERS OF MR. THAXTON
Vincinity Mechanicsburg, Ohio
Summer 1938

CREOLE TRAPPER'S CHILDREN
Plaquemines Parish, Louisiana
October 1935

SHARECROPPER'S CHILDREN ON SUNDAY
Little Rock, Arkansas
October 1935

SHARECROPPER'S CHILDREN ON SUNDAY
Little Rock, Arkansas
October 1935

COTTON PICKERS
Pulaski County, Arkansas
October 1935

69.

COTTON PICKERS
Pulaski County, Arkansas
October 1935

COTTON PICKERS
Pulaski County, Arkansas
October 1935

PICKING COTTON
Pulaski County, Arkansas
October 1935

72.

PICKING COTTON
Pulaski County, Arkansas
October 1935

73.

LOTTIE
Pulaski County, Arkansas
October 1935

COTTON PICKERS
Pulaski County, Arkansas
October 1935

75.

COTTON PICKERS
Pulaski County, Arkansas
October 1935

COTTON PICKERS
Pulaski County, Arkansas
October 1935

77.

COTTON PICKERS
Pulaski County, Arkansas
October 1935

78.

COTTON PICKERS
Pulaski County, Arkansas
October 1935

SHARECROPPER'S FAMILY
Little Rock, Arkansas
October 1935

SHARECROPPER'S WIFE AND CHILD
Little Rock, Arkansas
October 1935

SHARECROPPER'S FAMILY
Little Rock, Arkansas
October 1935

ROADSIDE SCENE
Liberty on Scott's Run, West Virginia
October 1935